T0073134

100 Questions and Answers to Help You Land Your Dream iOS Job

Or to Hire the Right Candidate!

Enrique López Mañas

Apress®

100 Questions and Answers to Help You Land Your Dream iOS Job: Or to Hire the Right Candidate!

Enrique López Mañas
München, Bayern, Germany

ISBN-13 (pbk): 978-1-4842-4272-8
https://doi.org/10.1007/978-1-4842-4273-5

ISBN-13 (electronic): 978-1-4842-4273-5

Library of Congress Control Number: 2018965463

Managing Director, Apress Media LLC: Welmoed Spahr
Acquisitions Editor: Natalie Pao
Development Editor: James Markham
Coordinating Editor: Jessica Vakili

Cover image designed by Freepik (www.freepik.com)

Distributed to the book trade worldwide by Springer Science+Business Media New York, 233 Spring Street, 6th Floor, New York, NY 10013. Phone 1-800-SPRINGER, fax (201) 348-4505, e-mail orders-ny@springer-sbm.com, or visit www.springeronline.com. Apress Media, LLC is a California LLC and the sole member (owner) is Springer Science+Business Media Finance Inc (SSBM Finance Inc). SSBM Finance Inc is a **Delaware** corporation.

For information on translations, please e-mail rights@apress.com, or visit www.apress.com/rights-permissions.

Apress titles may be purchased in bulk for academic, corporate, or promotional use. eBook versions and licenses are also available for most titles. For more information, reference our Print and eBook Bulk Sales web page at www.apress.com/bulk-sales.

Any source code or other supplementary material referenced by the author in this book is available to readers on GitHub via the book's product page, located at www.apress.com/978-1-4842-4272-8. For more detailed information, please visit www.apress.com/source-code.

Printed on acid-free paper

Table of Contents

About the Author

Enrique López Mañas is a Google Developer Expert and independent IT consultant. He has been working with mobile technologies and learning from them since 2007. He is an avid contributor to the open source community and a FLOSS (Free/Libre Open Source Software) kind of guy, being among the top-ten open source Java contributors in Germany. He is a part of the Google Launchpad accelerator team and participates in Google global initiatives to influence hundreds of the best startups from all across the globe. He is also a big data and machine learning aficionado.

In his free time, Enrique rides his bike, takes pictures, and travels until exhaustion. He also writes literature and enjoys all kinds of arts. He likes to write about himself in the third person. You can follow him on Twitter (@eenriquelopez) to stay informed on his latest activities.

Acknowledgments

This is my fourth published book. While on the fascinating journey of writing several books, I have discovered many things. One of the most important is that a book is rarely the result of the efforts of a single person. I could have not done it without the direct or indirect help of many talented and creative people.

My reviewers had a great impact and influence on the final state of this guide. Thanks to Adrian Kosmaczewski (a man capable of doing absolutely everything and whom you should follow on Medium), Bastian Kohlbauer, and Marian Zange, from whom I learn continually and improve my iOS craft. Pedro Piñera Buendía always is delightful company at all the events at which we meet and is an avid reader who inspires me, too, on Goodreads.

The folks from the Google Expert program upped my professional game to a level I could not have imagined. Working with them every day has changed my life in so many ways, and I am extremely happy to be a part of this community and contribute to it.

Many people in my personal life must be mentioned here, and many others will be left out, owing only to my poor memory: Marius, Mika, and Xavi, my longtime friends and colleagues from Barcelona; Gabriel Martínez, a computer-scientist-turned-designer, on whom I can always rely for professional and personal advice; Nick Skelton, a man who continually expanded my comfort zone. And everybody else who is and has been there for me during this undertaking.

Introduction

In 2015, I resigned from my previous position without another job. At the time, it felt scary—I was quitting a comfortable and secure post to pursue a different lifestyle, which I could not even define exactly. In retrospect, it turned out to be the best decision I made. I could focus on other projects; it got me out of my comfort zone; and it enabled me to push beyond boundaries I was never aware of.

At that time, I was conducting interviews for prospective candidates, and for that purpose, I ended up creating my own list of questions and answers. I tend to quantify and write notes and ideas meticulously in a daily journal, and so I did with all the questions. I also documented whether the candidates were able to respond to my questions, which directions the conversation took after a particular question, etc. Later, when I found myself on the opposite side of the desk, I realized that all the notes that I had organized and collected were of enormous value to me and that I had gained insights from my previous experience.

Eventually, I found a client, one with a challenging project (this is among the perks offered by mobile developers today, for which demand, especially for senior developers, significantly exceeds the supply of available workers). After a few intense weeks, which elucidated my future career path, I acquired several ideas. One recurrent thought was whether anyone in my situation could benefit from a well-organized book of potential interview questions categorized by job level. Another was whether a potential employer could use such a book to interview prospective employees. I had some spare time and had already compiled a list of questions, so I decided to publish the book *100 Questions and Answers to Help You Land Your Dream Android Job*.

It turned out to be a success, not financially, but I was rewarded in other ways. I began to receive messages from anonymous peers living in different parts of the world who shared real-life experiences. "Thank you for writing the book, I got an interview and passed it partially due to your help!" was one such message. Another was "I am relocating to the Bay Area from India with my family, and this book helped me to put my ideas in place." That pleased me greatly! As a mobile developer for many years, I was used to having limited interactions with people using my libraries and applications or reading my articles, but suddenly a book I wrote was having a real impact on the lives of others and their families. I felt empowered and in possession of a mission. I felt an obligation to continue doing this. Making a positive contribution to the world became a huge priority.

I conceived of writing this book almost immediately, but starting my life as a freelancer made me rethink my priorities: I ended up writing code for a very challenging project, but my free time rapidly declined, owing to other endeavors and responsibilities. Yet, the desire to write *100 Questions and Answers to Help You Land Your Dream iOS Job* intensified. So, day by day, I kept on writing (a question, an idea, etc.) until the book was complete. And, so, it is now in your hands or on your Kindle.

My purpose in writing this book is to help you land your dream iOS job, increase your knowledge of iOS, or help you, as an interviewer, to conduct effective interviews and make your life easier, in general. The questions are not very detailed, because this is not the purpose of the book. I do not think in an interview you need to go into extreme technical detail or be API-exact. Who remembers the parameters of a function? Or is knowing how to write compiling code in a whiteboard representative of any practical skills? I do not think so. I think an oral interview should be an informal discussion of APIs, a candidate's experience with frameworks and views on their advantages and disadvantages, sketching code, and being able to identify risks in particular scenarios. (I always liked to ask prospective candidates how they could create a memory leak, but I did not expect them to write a Java compiling class with no boilerplate code in a whiteboard. I would probably not have been able to do this myself!)

Some questions include a follow-up paragraph. When I am asking questions, if a candidate seems excited, very confident, or particularly keen on a subject, I like to discuss it further. This is an easy way to delve into the strengths and weaknesses of a particular field. For example, if a candidate is able to define a concurrency paradigm rather quickly, I will follow up by asking him or her to describe a good scenario in which to apply it. And maybe later we can also talk about mutability or how to securely store information in a device, if the course of the conversation moves in that direction.

If this book can truly help you in any way, I would appreciate you letting me know. If you have any constructive criticism that you want to share with me, I would appreciate it even more. If you find that the book was not useful or a waste of time, send me proof of payment, and I will reimburse you from the royalties I receive. (Depending on the provider, they can vary. For example, if you acquire this book on Google, I receive 70% of the total price.)

Last, but not least, happy coding! Be motivated in what you do daily and be the change that the world requires.

CHAPTER 1

Questions for a Junior Developer

The questions presented in this chapter are basic iOS questions. Senior developers should be very comfortable answering these, and junior developers, with up to one year of experience, should have knowledge of the relevant concepts.

This is by no means a bible. Feel free to select one of the questions, start an informal conversation with a friend or colleague, and observe the direction it takes. Depending on how the conversation branches, use your own sense and interests to decide to progress to the next question.

Question 1: What is a struct in iOS?

Structs are named types that allow for grouping items into one variable. A struct in Swift would look as follows:

```
struct SomeStruct {
        var name: String
        var attribute: String
}
```

© Enrique López Mañas 2019
E. López Mañas, *100 Questions and Answers to Help You Land Your Dream iOS Job*,
https://doi.org/10.1007/978-1-4842-4273-5_1

whereas in Objective-C, it would look like this:

```
struct City {
    NSString *name;
    NSString *attribute;
};
```

A good follow-up question for the candidate is to explain the difference between classes and structs, and where they can be more efficiently used. In Swift, structs are copied, and classes are referenced. Thus, they will be passed as values, not as references, in the case of large objects. Swift uses structs to improve performance, even with `String` and `Array` objects. Structs are preferable if

- The purpose is to encapsulate a few data values.

- The structure does not have to inherit values from other existing types.

Question 2: What is a framework in iOS?

A framework is a "skeleton" that has been packed in a bundle, to be used and distributed within other applications. A framework can contain a wide variety of extra resources (images, strings that already have been localized, data files, UI objects, etc.). Unless a framework has been released to the public, it generally contains the `.h` files that you need to run it, as well.

A good question with which to delve into this topic is to ask the candidate the difference between a framework and a library. A library can be defined as the collection of functionality ready to be linked and used in an application. The framework can be a library, a set containing many libraries, a collection of scripts, or whatever you need to create your application. It is a more abstract term. If the candidate is asked for particular examples, a library could be a networking library. A framework could be a plug-in manager or a GUI system.

Question 3: How can you store information within your iOS app?

iOS provides natively a few different ways to persist data in an application. They include

Keychain: This is thought to store sensitive data in a secure way (recurrent examples are logins and passwords).

SQLite database: If the data to be stored is complex or requires a huge amount of structured data, using an SQLite database is generally the best option.

Core Data: This is Apple's persistency framework. It's based on an object graph that describes the objects that should be saved. Then, you can directly work with these objects, and the framework takes care of saving it to a database.

Files: These can be directly saved in the application (for security reasons, an app can only access its own app container).

If you want to dive deeper, a potential candidate could discuss reasons for choosing SQLite over Core Data, for example. One reason could be that SQLite can be shared among different applications in other platforms, whereas Core Data is a framework exclusively available for Apple.

User Defaults: These can be used to persist a small amount of data. Typical examples are part of the configuration required to run the application. User defaults can persist the primitive types in iOS (`String`, `Data`, `Number`, `Date`, `Array`, and `Dictionary`).

Question 4: What is a dictionary? Is it similar to other structures in other programming languages?

A dictionary stores associations between keys belonging to the same type, and values also belonging to the same type, in a collection with no defined ordering. Each value is associated with a unique key, acting as an identifier for that value within the dictionary. It is similar to what is known in other languages as a HashMap, with some subtle differences.

Question 5: What is a provisioning profile?

A provisioning profile is a collection of digital entities that uniquely ties developers and devices to an authorized iPhone development team and enables a device to be used for testing. A development provisioning profile must be installed on each device on which you wish to run your application code.

If you want to discuss this further with a candidate, you can ask him or her about the signing process of an iOS application.

Question 6: What is ARC?

Automatic Reference Counting (ARC) is a compiler feature that provides automatic memory management for all your Objective-C objects. Instead of having to manually retain and release operations, ARC lets you focus on the part of the code that is more interesting, the object graphs, and the relationships between objects in your application.

Discussing ARC can veer into more interesting directions. If the candidate displays a solid profile, you might want to discuss the differences between traditional garbage collection methods. In the case of ARC, there is no background process deallocating objects at runtime, as in other technologies.

Question 7: What is Auto Layout?

Auto Layout is a means by which developers can create user interfaces, by defining relationships between elements. It provides a flexible and powerful system that describes how views and the UI controls relate to each other. By using Auto Layout, you can get an incredible degree of control over layout, with a wide range of customization, and yield the perfect interface.

Question 8: How do you manage dependencies in iOS?

Unlike other platforms, Apple does not officially provide any way to handle dependencies in an iOS project. As a de facto standard, CocoaPods is widely used among the iOS community. Dependencies for projects are specified in a single text file, called a Podfile, with which CocoaPods resolves dependencies between libraries, fetches the resulting source code, then links it together in an Xcode workspace to build your project.

A more experienced candidate could certainly mention another alternative to CocoaPods, namely, Carthage, which is quite popular and has been written in Swift.

Want to discuss this even further? Then start a discussion over the advantages of Carthage vs. CocoaPods.

Question 9: How do you debug and profile on iOS?

This is a very general question to elicit a single answer from a prospective candidate. To make things interesting, the candidate should be able to discuss instrumentation in iOS and crash logs. If you have a known bug in your application, it can be a good practice to let the developer open your environment and see how he/she navigates through its different instruments (CPU debugging, etc.).

Question 10: What is the difference between an App ID and a Bundle ID in iOS?

A Bundle ID is used to precisely identify a single app. The Bundle ID string must be a uniform type identifier (UTI) that contains only alphanumeric characters (A–Z, a–z, 0–9), hyphens (-), and periods (.). The string should be in reverse DNS format.

An App ID is a two-part string used to identify one or more apps from a single development team. The string consists of a Team ID and a Bundle ID search string, with a period (.) separating the two parts. The Team ID is supplied by Apple and is unique to a specific development team, while the Bundle ID search string is supplied by you to match either the Bundle ID of a single app or a set of Bundle IDs for a group of apps.

Why would Apple choose such a confusing nomenclature is a secret nobody has revealed yet.

Question 11: How does code signing work?

Code signing is the process of univocally signing an application to set up your own credentials (using a private-public key). The used key is stored locally on your Macintosh computer, and when you want to use other workstations to perform your development, the identity must be shared as well.

An old joke goes, "Tutorial to easily sign your iOS app in 75 steps." The process is not straightforward, and no matter how experienced you are, it is always easy to forget some of the steps. However, a developer should be able to outline the key steps of the process.

Note: this process is subject to change in the future, especially the particular steps.

1. You must first create a CSR file in your local computer. For that, you must employ the CSR file, using the keychain access program. With this process, some information has to be specified (such as a common name, e-mail address, encryption type, etc.). This file must be **securely stored**.

2. After this has been done, you must create a certificate in your developer program web site. At some point during the process, the assistant will prompt for the previously created CSR file. Then a certificate will be created and downloaded. With a double-click, it will be added automatically to your keychain. To work with it, this certificate must be on your machine.

Question 12: What is the difference between a frame and bounds?

The frame of a UIView in iOS is an imaginary rectangle relative to the location of the superview in which it is contained. On the other hand, the bound is the relative rectangle to its own coordinate system. Both items are expressed as a location with x, y as the starting points and a size indicated by width and height.

Question 13: How do you cast between types?

For Objective-C and Swift, the answer will be different. In general, and because Objective-C is a superset of the language C, typecasting works in a similar way. We could do the following to cast a type:

```
int i = (int)42.69f;
```

In the case of C, the precision during this cast would get lost.

Casting in Swift is slightly more complex, albeit powerful. We use what is denominated a type check operator (`is` and `as`) to verify if a certain variable belongs to a particular type. Following is an example:

```
var appleCount = 0
var orangeCount = 0

for item in Shop {
    if item is Apple {
        appleCount += 1
    } else if item is Orange {
        orangeCount += 1
    }
}
```

In this example, if the condition is fulfilled (the item is an Apple or the item is an Orange), the operator returns a value `true`, the evaluation is successful, and the code will continue executing. Note that this can get more complex if there are multiple types to be considered.

The operator `as` is very similar. Consider the following code snippet:

```
if let _ = item as? Apple ...
if item is Apple ...
```

Both of these are very similar, but in this case, the as operator will convert the resulting class to be used later (which is often the case).

If you want to follow up on this question, ask the candidate the difference between using as? and as!

Question 14: Which method would you call to find an object type?

Here again we have different options, depending on the language we are using.

In Objective-C, we would have to call the following function:

```
[name isKindOfClass:[NSString class]]
```

whereas in Swift, we could proceed as follows:

```
if object is String
```

In Swift, we have a bunch of additional options that can help us as well.

```
type(of:)
isKind(of:)
isMember(of:)
conforms(to:)
```

Question 15: What's the difference between #if and #ifdef?

#if works as a usual if.

```
#if __IPHONE_OS_VERSION_MAX_ALLOWED >= 30200
        if (UI_USER_INTERFACE_IDIOM() ==
        UIUserInterfaceIdiomPad) {
```

```
            return YES;
        }
    #endif
    return NO;
```

#ifdef means "if defined—some value or macros."

```
#ifdef    RKL_APPEND_TO_ICU_FUNCTIONS
#define RKL_ICU_FUNCTION_APPEND(x) _RKL_CONCAT(x, RKL_APPEND_
TO_ICU_FUNCTIONS)
#else  // RKL_APPEND_TO_ICU_FUNCTIONS
#define RKL_ICU_FUNCTION_APPEND(x) x
#endif // RKL_APPEND_TO_ICU_FUNCTIONS
```

Question 16: What are iOS compilers?

Compilers are a vast topic, and by no means could a junior developer explain them in detail. However, if you are working with iOS, you should be aware that there are different compilers that can be used in iOS and that they have gone through different periods of maturity. They are GCC, LLVM with Clang, and LLVM with GCC.

This conversation can be extended ad infinitum. If asked about the current state of the art, a knowledgeable candidate will tell you that, in short, there is no need for GCC, and instead, LLVM with Clang is the compiler that will cover all your needs. Details can be also given: LLVM compiles faster than GCC; the generated code will generally be faster and provides also more accurate error messages when the compilation is taking place.

Question 17: How can you keep different flavors for production and development releases?

There are different approaches that could be used here. An initial one could be to create different targets, each of them employing different `Info.plist` files. Each time a target is selected, a different `Info.plist` will be used, thereby being able to differentiate between different variables (for example, tokens, URLs, etc.).

One could also think of using bundle identifiers. Defining different preprocessor macros will control the conditional compilation of various chunks of code.

Alternatively, or in addition, you could put your build configuration settings (including the changing location of the `Info.plist` file) into `*.xcconfig` files and reference those in your project, info, and configurations areas. Then, you could build a different version of your app simply by changing your scheme. Putting build configuration settings into files is a huge win for configuration control too.

Question 18: What is the difference between viewDidLoad and viewDidAppear? Which one would you use to load data from a remote server and display it in the screen?

`viewDidLoad()` is called only one time, when the view controller has been initially loaded into memory. Generally, when we want to instantiate variables and build views that will be alive during the entire life cycle of the view controller, we do it here. However, the view is still not visible!

`viewDidAppear()` is called when the view is first prompted into the screen. This method can actually be called several times during the life cycle of a view controller. Let's think, for example, when a modal view controller is loaded and later dismissed. The view already has been loaded, but it will appear twice as a result. In this method, we typically perform layout actions, such as drawing into the UI, presenting modal screens, etc.

This is where you want to instantiate any instance variables and build any views that live for the entire life cycle of this view controller. However, the view is usually not visible at this point.

To answer the question, you want to load data from a remote server in the method `viewDidLoad`. That way, it is loaded once, not every time the view appears.

To follow up with a candidate, you could ask him/her what the effect of retaining things in the `viewDidAppear` is. The effect is that very likely memory leaks will occur, if the items are not released after a view has disappeared.

Question 19: How do you track bugs? What are your tools of choice?

Here, the candidate will want to talk about the tools of choice she/he might already know. A few of them to cite (with no endorsement to any particular company implied) are Apteligent (formerly Crittercism), Crashlytics/Fabric, HockeyApp, or the Apple platform itself (when distributed, you can see crashes in iTunes Connect).

Question 20: What is NSUserDefaults?

`NSUserDefaults` is a class that allows a developer to save settings, properties, and information that is related to the application or the user data. `NSUserDefaults` stores keys and their associated value. The following types can be stored with `NSUserDefaults`:

- `NSData`

- `NSString`

- `NSNumber`

- `NSDate`

- `NSArray`

- `NSDictionary`

Possible follow-up questions here could be the following: What are the differences from other storing mechanisms in iOS? Is it possible to store an image with `NSUserDefaults`? The answer is yes. An image can be transformed into Base64 and stored as an `NSString`. Another question is whether this would be an efficient use of `NSUserDefaults`.

In general, the candidate should be prompted to discuss the benefits and disadvantages of using `NSUserDefaults` as opposed to other storage types.

Question 21: How do you test your code? How do you make your code testable?

These are also important questions that can branch into many interesting tangents and will, we hope, let us know about the candidate's mindset and theoretical knowledge. A relevant discussion could be of the perks of having manual testing and automated testing. Each type of test has different pros and cons. Let's talk about automated testing.

- Tests can run rather quickly, because there is no need for a human.

- They can be cost-effective, if we make proper use of the tools for automation. They can be expensive in the short term but definitely lower costs in the long run.

13

- Everyone can see results. Tests can be reproduced, recorded, and saved.

- On the other hand, tools might have limitations, and we might be constrained to the development of our testing tool or API.

Manual testing can also have its own virtues and vices.

- In the short term, it lowers costs.

- It is more likely to uncover real user issues. Because automatic tests are automated, they will not test special edge use cases or improvise and test something not provided in the script.

- On the other hand, some tasks can be rather difficult to perform manually, at worst, repetitive, boring, and not at all stimulating.

A candidate also could be prompted with the question, Which testing frameworks do you use? XCTest is tightly coupled with Xcode, and, therefore, most developers should have at least a minimum theoretical idea of the framework. Other testing frameworks include Appium and Calabash. To dive deeper, you could discuss the advantages and disadvantages of each framework. This could be convenient way to align the knowledge of the candidate with the knowledge of a company, although a candidate should never be hired based only on the knowledge of frameworks he/she possesses but on his/her general attitude and reasoning. The frameworks of today will be in the museums of tomorrow.

Last, but not least, an interesting discussion on the topic is how to make code testable. Principles to create a testable code always make for interesting conversation, and among them, SOLID is a very good starting point.

Question 22: What is the difference between atomic and nonatomic properties? Which is the default for synthesized properties? When would you use one vs. the other?

Atomic is the default behavior. An atomic property will ensure that the present process is completed by the CPU, before another process accesses the variable. Obviously, it is not fast, as it ensures that the process is entirely complete.

Nonatomic behavior, on the other hand, is not the default behavior. It is faster for synthesized code, that is, for variables created using `@property` and `@synthesize`. They are not thread-safe, and using them may result in unexpected behavior, when two different processes access the same variable at the same time.

Question 23: What are "strong" and "weak" references? Why are they important, and how can they be used to help control memory management and avoid memory leaks?

A strong reference is one that occurs by default anytime that a variable is being created. There is an important property with reciprocal strong references, and it is that when this happens, a retain cycle occurs. In this situation, ARC will never be able to destroy the objects. This is described as being a *memory leak*.

These types of reciprocal and strong references should always be avoided. When this is not possible, using weak references can come to the rescue. If one of these references is declared as weak, the retain cycle will be broken, and, therefore, the memory leak will be avoided.

Question 24: What is your process for tracing and fixing a memory leak?

The best approach to this question is to provide the candidate with an existing project and a known memory leak and ask him/her to debug it.

Question 25: What six instruments are part of the standard iOS set?

Among them, a candidate should come up with the names of Leaks, Multicore, Time Profiler, Zombies, System Usage, UI Recorder, Activity Monitor, Allocations, Core Animation.

To follow up, functionality and particularities of each tool are good topics to delve into.

Question 26: How do I add resources to my app?

Under the Resource groups, just drag a file into it and select "Create Folder References for any added folders." That way, the file will be added automatically.

Question 27: What are blocks?

Blocks are a language-level feature added to C, Objective-C, and C++, which allow you to create distinct segments of code that can be passed around to methods or functions as if they were values.

Blocks are Objective-C objects, which means they can be added to such collections as NSArray or NSDictionary. They also have the ability to capture values from the enclosing scope, making them similar to closures or lambdas in other programming languages.

A candidate willing to explore this topic further could also say that the equivalent of blocks in Swift are closures. Closures are first-class objects, so they can be nested and passed around (like blocks in Objective-C). In Swift, functions are just a special case of closures.

Question 28: How do you insert a sanity check that will be disabled in release builds?

You could use an assertion code that only runs in a debug build. The following piece of code is an example:

```
#if defined(NDEBUG)
{
    // The assertion code below should be compiled out of
    existence in a release
    // build.  Log an error and abort the program if it is not.
    bool ok = true;
    NSCAssert(ok = false, @"NS assertions should be disabled
    but are not");
    if (!ok)
    {
```

```
        NSLog(@"Detected release build but NS_BLOCK_ASSERTIONS
        is not defined");
        return -1;
    }
}
#endif
```

Question 29: When are let and var appropriate in Swift?

The let keyword defines a constant.

```
let theAnswer = 42
```

theAnswer cannot be changed afterward. This is why anything optional or weak can't be written using let. The former has to change during runtime and must be written using var.

var defines an ordinary variable.

```
var president = "Lincoln"
```

Question 30: What is a protocol, how do you define your own, and when is it used?

Protocols are a way to specify a set of methods you want a class to implement if it wants to work with one of your classes. Delegates and data sources such as UITableViewDelegate and UITableViewDataSource are indeed protocols.

```
@protocol MyProtocol <NSObject>

- (void)aRequiredMethod;
```

```
@required
- (void)anotherRequiredMethod;

@optional
- (void)anOptionalMethod;

@end
```

@required specifies that the method *must* be implemented, whereas @optional lets the developer decide.

You then can specify that a class "conforms" to a protocol (implements the required methods) in the interface of the class, as follows:

```
@interface MyClass <MyProtocol>

@end
```

Question 31: What is MVC, how is it implemented in iOS, and does it have any alternatives?

MVC is a well-known design pattern that defines how each component must be implemented, how components communicate between each other, and where each functionality must reside. By default, Apple provides an implementation of the MVC pattern: the UIViews are the views in which the UI lives; the UIViewControllers support the controller that listens to the events and can, therefore, update the view according to our needs; and the model is the data that the application uses and that can reside in any object we create to store useful information.

There are many alternatives to MVC. A common one could be using MVVM with Reactive Cocoa. Other alternatives could include Viper and using functional reactive code.

A well-versed candidate will tell you what the difference is between a pattern and an architecture. Broadly, a pattern is a model to solve a recurring problem in the realm of computer science, whereas architecture is a set of rules and organization that defines how code must be structured to be maintainable and extendable.

Question 32: What are different ways in which you can specify the layout of elements in a UIView?

There are a few different techniques to specify a layout in an iOS app.

- We can use `InterfaceBuilder` to add an XIB file to our project. Later, this XIB file can be loaded from within our application code. `InterfaceBuilder` also allows us to create a storyboard.

- You can write your own code to use `NSLayoutConstraints`, to have elements in a view arranged by Auto Layout.

- You can create `CGRects` describing the exact coordinates for each element and pass them to UIView's `- (id)initWithFrame:(CGRect)frame` method.

Question 33: What format code is used to print a formatted message with NSString?

You would use the following:

```
NSLog(@"Message == %@",msg);
```

CHAPTER 2

Questions for Prospective Candidates Who Have Been Working with iOS for Some Time

The following chapter includes questions that are aimed at very experienced developers, typically with one, two, or three years of experience. They feel comfortable and familiar with the SDK and most of the libraries used for iOS development. They have probably been working on their own framework or architecture for iOS development and can identify complex problems and provide solutions for them.

© Enrique López Mañas 2019
E. López Mañas, *100 Questions and Answers to Help You Land Your Dream iOS Job*,
https://doi.org/10.1007/978-1-4842-4273-5_2

Question 34: How is memory management handled on iOS?

Every iOS developer who has been in the game for a while should be comfortable talking about this topic. A poor knowledge of memory management can lead to memory leaks, poor performance, and disappointed managers, investors, developers, and users.

An answer could start by pointing out that Swift uses automatic reference counting (ARC), which is essentially the same as in Objective-C. By default, all the references are strong references. Strong reference cycles can therefore occur, and this makes it impossible for ARC to deallocate the memory. This can be solved by using weak references.

This conversation can extend to talking about unowned references. Unowned references are used in values that are always expecting to be other than nil and must therefore be defined as non-optional.

Also, another possible aspect of the conversation could be a discussion of closures.

Question 35: What do you know about singletons? Where would you use one, and where would you not?

A singleton is simply a class that only allows a single instance. You can't re-up instances of a singleton class.

One reason that tends to come uprepeatedly on the Internet is that of a "logging" class. In this case, a singleton can be used instead of a single instance of a class, because a logging class usually must be used over and over again ad nauseam by every class in a project.

Question 36: How do you typically do networking?

This conversation can be very interesting and reveal many insights into a developer's approaches. A developer should mention architectures he/she has used and the patterns he/she relies on. These can include service layers, MVVM, UI data binding, dependency injection, or functional reactive programming.

Which libraries does the developer use? Developers come from different backgrounds and might be using AFNetworking, ReactiveCocoa... How does he/she ensure that data can be saved from the network? What is the process from the time the user clicks a UI component until the data is stored locally on a device? What classes are involved in the selected architecture? How would the developer prepare the application for offline use, and docs he/she approach caching? How would he/she define an ideal API for mobile. Is he/she aware of all the HTTP methods (PUT, POST, GET, DELETE) and when and how would he/she use them?

There are no right/wrong answers to the preceding questions. Rather, they present a golden opportunity to discuss with an experienced potential colleague approaches that could also serve you, by comparing your own processes with a prospective employer's.

Question 37: How would you download a JSON from a web server, serialize it, and save it in your local storage?

This question is partially derived from the previous one. Here, a developer could talk about frameworks that could be used. NSJSONSerialization is the framework provided by Apple, but it has some bugs and limitations. In particular, it has some issues with data validation and conversion.

A still better answer would be to mention third-party libraries (thinking here of ObjectMapper or Mantle). Additionally, a discussion on how to logically separate the process of JSON to Logical Entity and Logical Entity to Storage would also be relevant.

Question 38: What design patterns are you aware of in iOS and use?

Every developer being interviewed should be aware of MVC. This is the paradigm that iOS is built on top of. The more seniority a developer has, the more frameworks he/she will be able to discuss. Here, you could include MVVM, which helps developers to prevent Massive View Controllers. Also, a developer could explain the differences and advantages and disadvantages of different frameworks.

Question 39: How do you handle async tasks?

In order to handle async tasks, iOS provides a mechanism known as Grand Central Dispatch. To use this, you must create a queue (in this context, this is similar to a thread) and pass a block to `dispatch_async()`, to be performed in the background.

However, a few other mechanisms can be used in iOS.

- Callbacks

- Global queues

- Memory

- Multiple tasks/blocks

A developer might want to discuss when each of these alternatives could be used and its advantages and disadvantages.

Question 40: What is managed object context, and what kind of functionality does it provide?

A managed object context is represented with an instance of the class NSManagedObjectContext. A managed object context can be understood as a temporary scratch pad for a related collection of objects. This set of objects represents a consistent view of several persistent stores. A single managed object instance exists in one, and only one, context, but multiple copies of an object can exist in different contexts.

Key functionality provided by a managed object context includes

- Life-cycle management

- Notifications

- Concurrency

Question 41: Can you compare and contrast the different ways of achieving concurrency in OS X and iOS?

There are basically three ways of achieving concurrency in iOS.

- Using threads

- Dispatch queues

- Operation queues

If you are able to identify all of these, you might also want to discuss their various aspects and differences. A problem with the threads is that the responsibility of designing a scalable system is up to the developer. She/he must decide how many threads must be created and take care of adjusting this number manually under changing conditions.

Using GCD, this management responsibility is delegated to the system level. The developer's responsibility is just to define the task that must be executed and add them to the dispatch queue. This can generally make life easier.

An operation queue is the Cocoa equivalent of a concurrent dispatch queue and is implemented by the `NSOperationQueue` class. Unlike dispatch queues, operation queues are not limited to executing tasks in FIFO order and support the creation of complex execution-order graphs for your tasks.

Question 42: What are the different background modes in iOS?

The following are the possible background modes available in iOS:

- **Lay audio**: The app is able to reproduce background audio.

- **Location updates**: Callbacks are triggered anytime the location of the device changes.

- **Perform finite-length tasks**: This is the generic case of "backgrounding" in iOS, in which the app is running and performing an operation.

- **Voice over IP (VoIP)**: The application is running and performing a VoIP on the background.

Question 43: Can you list and explain the different types of iOS application states?

- **Not running**: The app has not been launched or was running but was terminated by the system.

- **Inactive**: The app is running in the foreground but is currently not receiving events. (It may be executing other code, however.) An app usually stays in this state only briefly, as it transitions to a different state.

- **Active**: The app is running in the foreground and is receiving events. This is the normal mode for foreground apps.

- **Background**: The app is in the background and executing code. Most apps enter this state briefly on their way to being suspended. However, an app that requests extra execution time may remain in this state for a period of time. In addition, an app being launched directly into the background enters this state instead of the inactive state. For information about how to execute code while in the background, see Background Execution `https://developer.apple.com/library/archive/documentation/iPhone/Conceptual/iPhoneOSProgrammingGuide/TheAppLifeCycle/TheAppLifeCycle.html`.

- **Suspended**: The app is in the background but is not executing code. The system moves apps to this state automatically and does not notify them before doing so. While suspended, an app remains in memory but does not execute any code. When a low-memory condition occurs, the system may purge suspended apps without notice, to make more space for the foreground app.

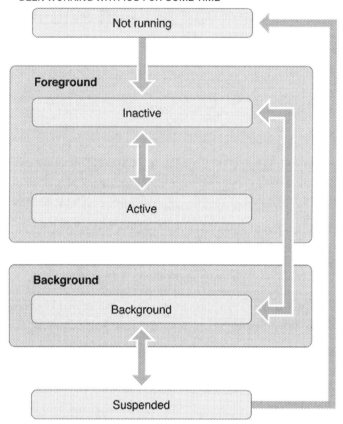

Figure 2-1. *iOS App lifecycle*

Question 44: What are the differences between copy and retain?

In a general setting, retaining an object will increase its retain count by one. This will help keep the object in memory and prevent it from being blown away. What this means is that if you only hold a retained version of an object, you share that copy with whoever passed it to you. Copying an object, however you do it, should create another object with duplicate values. Think of this as a clone. You do *not* share the clone with whoever passed it to you. When dealing with NSStrings in particular, you may not be able to assume that whoever is giving you an NSString is truly giving you an NSString. Someone could be handing you a subclass (NSMutableString, in this case), which means that they could potentially modify the values under the covers. If your application depends on the value passed in, and someone changes it, you could run into trouble.

Question 45: What can force an object destruction with ARC?

Just set the variables referencing those objects to nil. The compiler will then release the objects at that moment, and they will be destroyed, if no other strong references to them exists.

Question 46: What happens when you invoke a method on a nil pointer?

A message sent to a nil object is perfectly acceptable in Objective-C. It's treated as a no-op. There is no way to flag it as an error, because it's not an error. In fact, it can be a very useful feature of the language.

Question 47: When is it mandatory to synthetize properties?

When they are declared in protocols.

Question 48: What is NSAssert?

The NSAssert function is used to make sure that a value is what it's supposed to be. If an assertion fails, this means something has gone wrong, and so the app quits. One reason to use NSAssert would be if you have some function that will not behave or will create very bad side effects if one of the parameters passed to it is not exactly some value (or a range of values). In this case, you can put an NSAssert, to make sure that value is what you expect it to be. If it's not, something is really wrong, and so the app quits. NSAssert can be very useful for debugging/unit testing, and also when you provide frameworks to stop the users from doing "evil" things.

Question 49: What is a category in iOS?

Objective-C categories let you extend an existing class with whatever method you deem fit. It is pretty useful for adding helper methods to other classes that help parse the date in a way the class perhaps did not intend. You can also use it to split your own classes, so that if you have some big omni-class that does several things, you can opt in only the parts you want, by only including those categories.

Question 50: What could you use to add a new method to NSString?

Related to the previous question, the answer would be categories. To add a new method to an NSString, the answer would be to use a category. For example:

```
@interface NSString (CategoryName)

-(NSString *) aNewMethod;

@end
```

Question 51: What's your preference when writing UIs: XIB files, storyboards, or programmatic UIView?

There are arguments supporting each of the different models. It would be presumptuous to pretend to have a definitive answer. Instead, this question aims to discuss with a candidate his/her thinking and reasons for preferring one or another alternative (or which scenario they fit better). A possible answer could relate the advantages and disadvantages of each mechanism, for example:

Advantages of XIB files:

- You can quickly put together a UI.

- Provides straightforward implementation for small apps with a minimal number of screens.

- You can have separate XIBs for different localizations (i.e., languages or countries).

- They are great at laying out elements and visually spotting misalignments. They make it easy to make slight adjustments to the layout.

Disadvantages of XIB files:

- It's difficult to merge conflicts when working in a team environment (hard to diff, merge, and read).

- Highly dynamic views are impossible to describe as an XIB.

- Performance wise, they are slower than creating views through code, because the XIB has to be read from the disk and analyzed/parsed.

31

- XIBs lack customizations that you can do in code, such as Quartz stuff (drop shadows, round corners).

- They are harder to debug (i.e., if you forget to make a connection in Interface Builder or make a wrong connection).

Advantages of storyboards:

- Storyboards are nice for apps with a small to medium number of screens and relatively straightforward requirements for navigation between views.

- You can mock up the flow of an application without writing much, if any, code.

Disadvantages of storyboards:

- Storyboards are not compatible with pre-iOS 5, so they make supporting iOS 4.3 impossible.

- It's hard to work in parallel in a team environment, because everyone's modifying the same file.

- Along the same lines, merging conflicted storyboards in GIT will be a pain.

- With storyboards, people have experienced bugs in Xcode (e.g., having to frequently flush the `DerivedData` folder because of inconsistencies).

Advantages of views created programmatically:

- It's easier to merge conflicts and diff lines of code than with an XIB file.

- You can trace through code when debugging and not have to look at Interface Builder.

- Performance wise, it offers faster view creation than XIBs.

- Creating views through code gives you more control and free rein.

Disadvantages with views created programmatically:

- It's harder to visualize the UI and gain a mental picture of what it will look like, if all your UI creation doesn't happen in one place in your code.

- You can't visually position elements, making it more time-consuming to lay out your views.

- It will take newcomers to your project team longer to grasp the app flow and navigation.

Question 52: How would you securely store private user data offline on a device? What other security best practices should be taken?

There is no right answer to these questions, but they're a great way to see how much a person has dug into iOS security. Especially if interviewing with banks or other entities in which security is paramount, these kinds of questions should be expected. I have no strict guidelines for an answer, but at least a few of the following topics should be discussed:

- If the data is extremely sensitive, it should never be stored offline on the device, because all devices are crackable.

- The keychain is one option for storing data securely. However, its encryption is based on the pin code of the device. Users are not forced to set a pin, so in some situations, the data may not even be encrypted. In addition, users' pin codes may be easily hacked.

- A better solution is to use something like SQLCipher, which is a fully encrypted SQLite database. The encryption key can be enforced by the application and separate from the user's pin code.

- Only communicate with remote servers over SSL/ HTTPS.

- If possible, implement certificate pinning in the application, to prevent man-in-the-middle attacks on public Wi-Fi.

- Clear sensitive data out of memory by overwriting it.

- Ensure that all validation of data being submitted is also run on the server side.

Question 53: Have you ever worked with NSOperationQueue? Can you explain it?

One way to perform operations concurrently in iOS is with the NSOperation and NSOperationQueue classes. NSOperationQueue regulates the concurrent execution of operations. It acts as a priority queue, such that operations are executed in a roughly FIFO manner, with higher-priority (NSOperation.queuePriority) ones getting to jump ahead of lower-priority ones. NSOperationQueue can also limit the maximum number of concurrent operations to be executed at any given moment, using the maxConcurrentOperationCount property.

Question 54: How would you serialize an array to disk?

The key classes to be used are an abstract class called NSCoder, along with a protocol called NSCoding. Together, these are designed to standardize the process of converting classes to and from serialized data formats. You've probably come across NSCoding in some capacity if you've ever used NIB files or storyboards, because NSCoding is the underlying mechanism that Cocoa uses for loading views and view controllers from NIBs.

Question 55: How does instancetype work, and how is it useful?

instancetype is a contextual keyword that can be used as a result type to signal that a method returns a related result type. For example:

```
@interface Person
+ (instancetype)personWithName:(NSString *)name;
@end
```

To evaluate the learning curve of a candidate, a follow-up question could be to discuss the similarities and differences between using instancetype and id. instancetype, unlike id, can only be used as the result type in a method declaration.

Question 56: What does the term *reflection* mean?

Reflection refers to the code that is able to inspect itself or some other code in the system. Objective-C has reflection (and abstract classes). A follow-up question to a prospective candidate would be When does reflection suit our needs?

Question 57: What are layer objects, and what do they represent?

Layer objects are data objects that represent visual content. Layer objects are used by views to render their content. Custom layer objects can also be added to the interface, to implement complex animations and other types of sophisticated visual effects.

Question 58: In Swift enumerations, what's the difference between raw values and associated values?

Raw values are for when every case in the enumeration is represented by a compile-time-set value. The are akin to constants, for example:

```
enum E: Int {
    case A  // if you don't specify, IntegerLiteralConvertible-
            based enums start at 0
    case B
}
```

In this case, A will have the value 0, and B will have the value 1.

Associated values are more like variables, associated with one of the enumeration cases.

```
enum E {
    case A(Int)
    case B
    case C(String)
}
```

Question 59: What does @synthesize do?

`@synthesize` creates a getter and a setter for the variable. This allows you to specify some attributes for your variables, and when you `@synthesize` that property to the variable, you generate the getter and setter for the variable.

The property name can be the same as the variable name. Sometimes people want it to be different, so as to use it in `init` or `dealloc` or when the parameter is passed with the same variable's name.

Question 60: What are the collection types available in Swift?

In Swift, collection types come in two varieties: `Array` and `Dictionary`.

`Array`: You can create an array of a single type or an array with multiple types. Swift usually prefers the former. Following is an example of a single-type array:

```
var cardName : [String] = [ "Robert" , "Lisa" ,
"Kevin"]
```

To add an array, you must use the subscript

```
println(CardNames[0]).
```

`Dictionary`: This is similar to a hash table in other programming language. A dictionary enables you to store key-value pairs and access the value by providing the key, as in the following example:

```
var cards = [ "Robert": 22, "Lisa" : 24, "Kevin": 26]
```

Question 61: What is a custom operator in Swift?

Custom operators in Swift are handy when you want a completely new operator, typically, because the functionality is so unique that none of the current operators makes sense. The next interesting question for the potential candidate is which types of custom operators exist in Swift. He/she should be able to come up with the following list:

> **Prefix**: A unary (operating on one value) operator that is just *before* the value it operates on.

> **Postfix**: A unary operator that is just *after* the value it operates on.

> **Infix**: A binary (operating on two values) operator placed *between* the two values it operates on.

As a coding exercise, a candidate could write the custom operator for a particular problem.

Question 62: What issues are you are aware of when working with blocks?

Blocks in iOS can introduce retain cycles in particular circumstances. This can happen especially if you fail to avoid strong references cycles when capturing self.

Question 63: What is an iOS extension?

Swift extensions basically add methods to existing types (classes, structures, and enumerations), only in a few different "flavors."

The following code creates an extension for the class `UIColor`.
Note that the keyword being used here is `extension`, rather than `class`,
`struct`, or `enum`.

```
extension UIColor: ImportantProtocol,
MoreImportantCustomProtocol {

}
```

Question 64: What is application sandboxing?

App Sandbox is an access control technology provided in OS X, enforced at the kernel level. It is designed to contain damage to the system and the user's data, if an app becomes compromised. Apps distributed through the Mac App Store must adopt App Sandbox. Apps signed and distributed outside of the Mac App Store with Developer ID can (and, in most cases, should) use App Sandbox as well.

For security reasons, iOS places each app (including its preferences and data) in a sandbox at install time. A sandbox is a set of fine-grained controls that limit the app's access to files, preferences, network resources, hardware, and so on. As part of the sandboxing process, the system installs each app in its own sandbox directory, which acts as the home for the app and its data.

Question 65: How do you develop applications for iPad and iPhone?

If you select Device family as universal, when creating a new project, you will receive options to prepare different XIB files or storyboards for iPhone and iPad. At a code level, you can either check for the device or use proper naming while allocating it.

At runtime, you might want to load some resources, depending on whether the device is an iPhone or iPad. From a programmatic code perspective, you could proceed as follows (in Swift):

```swift
switch UIDevice.currentDevice().userInterfaceIdiom {
    case .Phone:
    // It's an iPhone
    case .Pad:
    // It's an iPad
    case .Unspecified:
    //
}
```

Question 66: What are the different background modes in iOS?

- **Play audio**: The app can continue playing and/or recording audio in the background.

- **Receive location updates**: The app can continue to get callbacks as the device's location changes.

- **Perform finite-length tasks**: This is the generic "whatever" case, in which the app can run arbitrary code for a limited amount of time.

- **Process Newsstand Kit downloads**: Specific to Newsstand apps, the app can download content in the background.

- **Provide voice over IP (VoIP) services**: The app can run any arbitrary code in the background. Of course, Apple limits its use, so that your app must provide VoIP service too.

CHAPTER 3

We Need That Person on Board to Do Great Things!

This chapter is dedicated to upper-level iOS engineers—typically, those with several years of experience and who have worked on a wide range of projects with a greater number of requirements. Remember that experience must be combined with practical analytical and problem-solving skills. Employers won't want to hire a candidate who just read this book and memorized it, for example.

Especially with the questions in this chapter, you want to promote discussion and the exchange of opinions. Sometimes, there is a single solution to real-time problems, and most of these solutions involve a trade-off. You may have to give up in performance what you gain in code usability, etc.

Senior developers also require the leadership and motivational skills to lead a team. This book does not cover possible questions or methods to identify those skills, but I am sure the reader already has some idea about how to identify these. Senior developers must be comfortable and self-confident when discussing any topic, and they should be able to embrace change. They should have an entrepreneurial aura about them. They are facilitators rather than bosses and should encourage independence and freethinking.

© Enrique López Mañas 2019
E. López Mañas, *100 Questions and Answers to Help You Land Your Dream iOS Job*,
https://doi.org/10.1007/978-1-4842-4273-5_3

Question 67: What is the difference between delegation and KVO?

Both are ways to create relationships between objects. Delegation is a one-to-one relationship in which one object implements a delegate protocol and another uses it and sends messages, assuming that those methods are implemented, because the receiver promises to comply to the protocol. KVO is a many-to-many relationship in which one object can broadcast a message, and one or multiple other objects can listen and react to it.

Question 68: What is method swizzling? When would you use it?

Method swizzling is the process of changing the implementation of an existing selector. It's a technique made possible by the fact that method invocations in Objective-C can be changed at runtime, by changing how selectors are mapped to underlying functions in a class's dispatch table.

For example, let's say we wanted to track how many times each view controller is presented to a user in an iOS app. Each view controller could add tracking code to its own implementation of viewDidAppear:, but that would make for a ton of duplicated boilerplate code. Subclassing would be another possibility, but it would require subclassing UIViewController, UITableViewController, UINavigationController, and every other view controller class—an approach that would also suffer from code duplication.

Question 69: Take three objects: a grandparent, parent, and child. The grandparent retains the parent, the parent retains the child, and the child retains the parent. The grandparent releases the parent. What happens?

A retain cycle happens. Because they are retained, it will not be possible to release them from memory. This can be solved by making one of the references weak.

Question 70: What are two separate and independent reasons why-retainCount should never be used in shipping code?

You should never use -retainCount, because it never tells you anything useful. The implementation of the Foundation and AppKit/UIKit frameworks is opaque. You don't know what's being retained, why it's being retained, who's retaining it, when it was retained, and so on. Following are examples of when to use -retainCount:

- [NSNumber numberWithInt:1] now has a retainCount of 9223372036854775807. If your code was expecting it to be 2, your code has now broken.

- You'd think that @"Foo" would have a retainCount of 1. It doesn't. It's 1152921504606846975.

- You'd think that [NSString stringWithString:@"Foo"] would have a retainCount of 1. It doesn't. Again, it's 1152921504606846975.

Basically, because anything can retain an object (and, therefore, alter its `retainCount`), and because you don't have the source to most of the code that runs an application, an object's `retainCount` is meaningless. If you're trying to track down why an object isn't getting deallocated, use the leaks tool in Instruments. If you're trying to track down why an object was deallocated too soon, use the zombies tool in Instruments. But don't use `-retainCount`. It's a truly worthless method.

Question 71: How does an autorelease pool work at the runtime level?

Every time `-autorelease` is sent to an object, it is added to the innermost autorelease pool. When the pool is drained, it simply sends `-release` to all the objects in the pool.

Autorelease pools are simply a convenience that allows you to defer sending `-release` until "later." That "later" can happen in several places, but the most common in Cocoa GUI apps is at the end of the current run loop cycle.

Question 72: Which is faster: to iterate through an NSArray or an NSDictionary?

When the order of the items in the collection is not important, sets offer better performance for finding items in the collection. The reason is that a set uses hash values to find items (like a dictionary), while an array has to iterate over its entire contents to find a particular object.

Figure 3-1 shows a very representative image of the Apple documentation stating this.

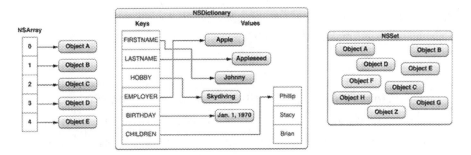

Figure 3-1. *Object collection framework in iOS*

Question 73: Which is faster: to iterate through an NSArray or an NSSet?

NSArray is faster than NSSet for simply holding and iterating. On the lower end, it is as much as 50% faster for constructing and, at the higher end, as much as 500% faster for iterating. If you are required only to iterate content, don't use NSSet.

Question 74: Do you have to implement all the declarations from an adopted protocol?

No. If a method is declared as @optional, it does not have to be implemented.

@protocol MyProtocol

- (void)requiredMethod;

@optional
- (void)anOptionalMethod;
- (void)anotherOptionalMethod;

```
@required
- (void)anotherRequiredMethod;
```

```
@end
```

If a developer is asked to identify a risk with this approach, he/she should be able to advance the idea that if a method in a protocol is marked as optional, you must check whether an object implements that method, before attempting to call it.

Question 75: What is a shortcut for calling alloc and init?

alloc and init can generally be called like this:

```
[[Class alloc] init]
```

In some other pieces of code and in the literature, we can also find the following:

```
[Class new]
```

Originally in Objective-C, objects were created with new. As the OpenStep/Cocoa framework evolved, designers formed the opinion that allocating the memory for an object and initializing its attributes were separate concerns and, thus, should be separate methods (for example, an object might be allocated in a specific memory zone). So, the alloc-init style of object creation came into favor. Basically, new is old and almost-but-not-quite deprecated. Therefore, you'll see that Cocoa classes have a lot of init methods but almost never any custom new methods.

Question 76: What kind of pointer can help to safely avoid a memory leak?

Smart pointers can be very helpful in automating the bookkeeping of object lifetimes. A smart pointer is a class that wraps a "raw" (or "bare") C++ pointer, to manage the lifetime of the object being pointed to. There is no single smart pointer type, but all of them try to abstract a raw pointer in a practical way.

Smart pointers should be preferred over raw pointers. If you feel you must use pointers (first consider if you really do), you would normally want to use a smart pointer, as this can alleviate many of the problems with raw pointers, mainly, forgetting to delete the object and leaking memory.

Question 77: What can help to prevent an out-of-memory crash if you have a long-running execution loop?

Here, one key is memory leaks. Make sure that the memory is being cleaned and you are not keeping any references that prevent an object from being collected. Look also for the applicationWillTerminate message in your app delegate. This is called if your app is terminated by the system (e.g., owing to low memory) but not if the user leaves the app in the usual way, by pressing the home key.

Question 78: What are the requisite considerations when writing a UITableViewController that shows images downloaded from a remote server?

By itself, programming this feature can be a coding task for a prospective candidate. However, if the question is asked orally, the candidate should answer by citing some general guidelines on how to deal with the aspect of storage and asynchronicity derived from this problem. Some of the points to cover are

- Only download the image when the cell is scrolled into view, i.e., when `cellForRowAtIndexPath` is called.

- Download the image asynchronously on a background thread, so as not to block the UI, so the user can keep scrolling.

- When the image has downloaded for a cell, we must check if that cell is still in the view or whether it has been reused by another piece of data. If it's been reused, we should discard the image. Otherwise, we must switch back to the main thread, to change the image on the cell.

Depending on the accuracy of the conversation, you might want to steer this discussion toward how images can be cached for a later offline user, usage of placeholders, etc.

Question 79: What is KVC and KVO? What is an example of using KVC to set a value?

KVC stands for "key-value coding." It's a mechanism by which an object's properties can be accessed using strings at runtime, rather than having to statically know the property names at development time. KVO stands for "key-value observing" and allows a controller or class to observe changes to a property value.

For example, if there is a property name on a class

```
@property (nonatomic, copy) NSString *name;
```

we can access it using KVC, as follows:

```
NSString *n = [object valueForKey:@"name"]
```

and we can modify its value by sending it the following message:

```
[object setValue:@"Mary" forKey:@"name"]
```

Question 80: What mechanisms does iOS provide to support multi-threading?

There are a bunch of different techniques that we can use in iOS to provide multi-threading to an application.

- NSThread creates a new low-level thread that can be started by calling the start method.

- NSOperationQueue allows a pool of threads to be created and used to execute NSOperations in parallel. NSOperations can also be run on the main thread by asking NSOperationQueue for the mainQueue.

- Grand Central Dispatch (GCD) is a modern feature of Objective-C that provides a rich set of methods and APIs to use to support common multi-threading tasks. GCD provides a way to queue tasks for dispatch on either the main thread, a concurrent queue (tasks are run in parallel), or a serial queue (tasks are run in FIFO order).

Question 81: What is the responder chain?

When an event occurs in a view, for example, a touch event, the view will fire the event to a chain of `UIResponder` objects associated with the `UIView` class. The first `UIResponder` is `UIView` itself. If it does not handle the event, it continues up the chain until `UIResponder` handles it. The chain will include `UIViewControllers`, parent `UIViews`, and their associated `UIViewControllers`. If none of those handles the event, then the `UIWindow` is asked if it can handle it, and, finally, if that doesn't handle the event, the `UIApplicationDelegate` is asked.

Because this is all quite hierarchical, a candidate could be asked to draw this on a whiteboard. A diagram similar to Figure 3-2 will nail the problem.

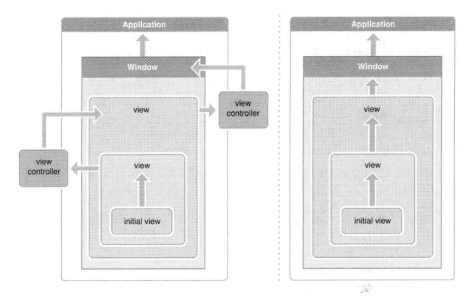

Figure 3-2. *Responder chain flow in iOS*

Question 82: What is the difference between using a delegate and notification?

You can think of delegates as being like a telephone call. You call up your buddy and specifically want to talk to her. You can say something, and she can respond. You can talk until you hang up the phone. Delegates, in much the same way, create a link between two objects, and you don't have to know what type the delegate is; it simply has to implement the protocol.

On the other hand, NSNotification is like a radio station. It broadcasts messages to whoever is willing to listen. A radio station can't receive feedback from its listeners, unless it has a telephone (delegate). Listeners can ignore a message, or they can do something with it. NSNotification allows you to send a message to any object, but without a link between them to communicate back and forth. If you require this type of communication, you should probably implement a delegate; otherwise, NSNotification is simpler and easier to use, although it may get you into trouble.

Question 83: How would you securely store private user data offline on a device? What other security best practices should be taken?

This question should trigger a conversation with the candidate about best practices and frameworks. A well-versed candidate will be able to talk about Keychain, Touch ID, and 1password. In addition, general conversations about network security (using SSL connections, using Charles for debugging, and so forth) can lead to interesting places.

Question 84: Are SQL injection attacks valid in iOS? How would you prevent them?

SQL injection attacks are very likely to occur in iOS. There are a few ways to prevent them. One is to use parameterized queries.

Question 85: What are the common reasons for app rejections in the App Store?

I particularly like this question, although is not technical. A person who has been in the iOS development arena for a while will likely have witnessed several rejections. From these, you can elicit interesting stories from the candidate and also analyze how he/she approaches and solves those problems.

Question 86: How can you make a code snippet thread safe?

You can use the keyword @synchronized. This will automatically make a thread safe.

There is a very interesting approach that few engineers might be familiar with, and if a candidate can mention it, he/she is definitely on his/her game: making all objects immutable, so that they cannot be modified.

Question 87: Why should we release the outlets in viewDidUnload?

viewDidUnload is strictly used for releasing IBOutlets with retain properties. The reason for this has to do with the fact that UIViewController has a view property that it retains. That view property itself retains references to all of its subviews. These subviews are exactly what you are retaining inside these outlet properties. The problem lies in that these subviews have an "extra" retain.

The goal of -viewDidUnload is to clear up unnecessary memory usage. When -viewDidUnload is called, the view property has already been released, which releases the top level UIView, along with all its subviews. Because we have retained some of these subviews, however, they linger in memory, and we want to release them, because they will no longer be used. New copies of these subviews will be created when (if) the view is reloaded. The properties are also set to nil, strictly, so we don't have pointers pointing to deallocated memory.

Question 88: What is the difference between a shallow copy and a deep copy?

Shallow copies duplicate as little as possible. A shallow copy of a collection is a copy of the collection structure, not the elements. With a shallow copy, two collections now share the individual elements.

Deep copies duplicate everything. A deep copy of a collection is two collections with all of the elements in the original collection duplicate.

Question 89: How would you pass an unknown type as a parameter?

You could use (id).

```
-(void) fooMethod:(id)unknownTypeParameter {
    if( [unknownTypeParameter isKindOfClass:[Animal Class]]) {
        Animal *referanceObj = (Animal *) unknownTypeParameter;
        referanceObj.noOfLegs = 4;
    }
}
```

Question 90: What is deinitializer and how it is written in Swift?

A deinitializer is declared immediately before a class instance is deallocated. You write a deinitializer with the deinit keyword. A deinitializer is written without parentheses, and it does not take any parameters. It is written as follows:

```
deinit {
        // perform the deinitialization
}
```

Question 91: What is optional chaining?

The process of querying—calling properties, subscripts, and methods on an optional that may be nil—is defined as optional chaining. Optional chaining return two values:

- If the optional contains a value, calling its related property, methods, and subscripts returns value.

- If the optional contains a nil value, all its related properties, methods, and subscripts return nil.

Because multiple queries to methods, properties, and subscripts are grouped, failure of one chain will affect the entire chain and result in a nil value.

Question 92: What is the Fallthrough statement? What does it do?

Fallthrough "falls through" to the next case, not to the next matching case. The concept is inherited from C switch statements, in which each case may be thought of as a go-to destination label, and the switch statement brings execution to the first matching one.

Question 93: What are lazy stored properties and when are they useful?

Lazy stored properties are used for a property whose initial values are not calculated until the first time it is used. You can declare a lazy stored property by writing the lazy modifier before its declaration. Lazy properties are useful when the initial value of a property relies on outside factors whose values are unknown.

Question 94: Have you heard of Handoff?

Handoff is a new feature introduced with iOS 8 and OS X Yosemite. Handoff allows you to continue an activity uninterrupted when you switch from one device to another, without the need to reconfigure either device.

Question 95: Can you have more UIWindows in iOS?

It is a rare case, although it is possible. For example, this happens when you have a `UIAlertView` in a separate window.

Question 96: What is Metal?

Metal is a low-level, less portable, more optimized graphics layer for doing the same kind of things you would with OpenGL (and OpenCL) or Direct3D, that is, 3D graphics rendering and parallel GPU programming. Metal attempts to lower the amount of overhead required for performance reasons, as well as reduce CPU bottlenecks.

Question 97: Can you come up with strategies to increase efficiency in your networking?

An experienced developer should know some techniques not available by default in iOS. This will up your game.

You could discuss such topics as latency gauging (evaluating the type of network you are connected to, in order to make a decision about the data transmission), batching (packing requests together and sending them along when they are a representative group—something done in many analytics SDKs), pre-fetching (downloading information when the device is idle or the Internet connection is strong), exponential back-off (if a connection fails, wait for exponentially increasing intervals before making the next request), caching mechanisms, usage of Last-Modified headers...

Question 98: What is the most complex problem you had to solve at your previous job?

This question will reveal skills the candidate possesses that are unrelated directly to iOS knowledge but equally important. This can direct you to discuss the problems of growing an application, escalating a system, how to make software grow sustainably in the long term, how to grow teams and make them work efficiently, and frameworks the candidate has used to solve problems.

Question 99: What is an autorelease pool?

The `NSAutoreleasePool` class is used to support Cocoa's reference-counted memory management system. An autorelease pool stores objects that are sent a release message when the pool itself is drained. Also, if you use automatic reference counting, you cannot use autorelease pools directly. Instead, you use `@autoreleasepool` blocks.

Question 100: What is the class hierarchy from a UIButton to an NSObject?

UIButton inherits from UIControl, UIControl inherits from UIView, UIView inherits from UIResponder, UIResponder inherits from the root class NSObject: UIButton ➤ UIControl ➤ UIView ➤ UIResponder ➤ NSObject.

Can I ask you for a favor?

If you enjoyed this book and/or found it informative or otherwise useful, I'd really appreciate it if you posted a short review on Amazon. I read all the reviews, so that I can continue to write about what people are interested in.

Feedback, corrections, questions, doubts, suggestions? Feel free to contact me via e-mail at eenriquelopez@gmail.com.

Thank you for your support!

Printed in the United States
By Bookmasters